THE LAW OF HONOR

Dr. Clarice Fluitt

The Law of Honor © 2014 Clarice Fluitt

Unless otherwise noted, all Scripture quotations are from the King James Version of the Bible. All underscoring, parenthetical notes, bold lettering, and literal definitions of the Scriptures in this text are supplied by this author with appropriate modern renditions substituted for easy reading. Additional reference resources include: Hebrew and Greek Definitions; Strong's Exhaustive Concordance; Vines Expository Dictionary.

ISBN: 0990369404

Publisher: Clarice Fluitt Enterprises, LLC

Cover Design by:
Dokia Design
|443-721-1350|info@dokiadesign.com

Dedication

To my grandmother Lonie Banks who, on her death bed, dedicated to the Lord her entire family and generations to come.

To a preacher named "Daddy Flowers." He explained to my mother, who was orphaned at the age of 5, that there was a loving God. This caring God wanted her to know Him and spend forever in heaven with Him without being in pain or being lonely and rejected.

To my father and mother who taught me what honor is.

To FRIEND: When I was 5 years old, a Man dressed in a white robe and a large gold belt came down the stairs from heaven, walked over to me while I was making mud pies under a gum ball tree, smiled, and asked what I was doing. I replied, "Making stuff out of dirt." He laughed and said He had done that before. I asked Him His name. He said, "Call Me Friend." That was my first encounter with Jesus. He has been my faithful and best friend all of my life.

Acknowledgments

Every act of gratitude is a refinement to our soul.

I have been extremely blessed to have had so many excellent and enriching friendships that have served to inform and transform my life. Among these great treasures are my dear friends Apostle Donald Peart, his beautiful and gifted wife Prophetess Judith, and their anointed family. Their vision and formatting for this book are what made it possible. To my brilliant staff that faithfully plow through every challenge; Dr. Tandie Mazule, my Executive Assistant, and Dr. Evon Peet, my Administrative Assistant, who both spent many hours, days, and nights proofreading and editing this work. Only eternity will reveal how your callings and election have changed the world. You are champions.

I cannot begin to thank all those who have been a positive influence to me through the years, but each and every one contributed to my understanding of the power that is released when we choose to appropriate the fullness of The Law of Honor in our lives.

Endorsements

Dr. Clarice Fluitt is one of the most amazing women I have ever met. She has consistently encouraged leaders, executives, and those hungry to grow in the realization of their dreams and visions. Dr. Clarice believes in the God who makes all things possible. I have personally been mentored and coached by her and as a result, my life is much richer and fuller for every moment she has invested into me. She is one of my "heroes" — a woman of great love and faith!

Patricia King: She is a respected minister of the gospel, *Life Coach, and Founder of XP Ministries*

Dr. Clarice Fluitt is by far one of the most captivating speakers I have ever encountered. She has the unique gift of being able to unpack inspiration and insight in a humorous, inspiring, practical and personal way that few people can accomplish. The wisdom she shares from her incredible life experiences is simply transformational. She will literally keep you on the edge of your seat and challenge you to rethink your worldview and mindset in ways you never imagined. She will make you laugh until your ribs hurt, and move your spirit in a deep and profound way.

Kendra Todd: She was the youngest woman to *win NBC's The Apprentice with Donald Trump.*

She is not only an international television celebrity and real estate mogul, but is the consummate role model for professional women.

Table of Contents

Preface

From Genesis to Revelation, from the beginning of time until now, the absence of honor toward God and His Holy Word has been the seedbed of all decline.

God requires honor from His family in His Commandments and Ordinances. In exchange, He extends our lives and prospers our hands.

This book examines the absolute need for the believer to esteem, reverence, and honor God. It is our responsibility and privilege to exemplify the principle of the Law of Honor for our sake, and for the benefit of all generations to come.

Consider the Scripture verses that command us to show honor and respect:

To God	Revelation 4:11
To parents	Ephesians 6:2-3
To employers	1 Timothy 6:1
To believers	Romans 12:10
To leaders	1 Timothy 2:1-2
To everyone	1 Peter 2:17

Introduction
Honor Defined

What is it? Where does it come from? Is it a natural instinct or supernaturally imposed? How does one get it? Where does one put it? What does it look like? Does it have a sound? How does one carry it and how, if at all, do I benefit from it?

While honor has a broad range of uses, its definition can be narrowed down to that of character, integrity, and high esteem toward God, and toward others. Those whose lives exemplify submission, service, virtue, and wisdom carry the pattern that defines honor in its truest sense.

The law of honor is one of the most important laws on earth. I can relate the story of a little boy I knew who had a great challenge in his life honoring anything bigger than himself. He was very possessive of what was his. It did not come instinctively to say yes sir, no sir, thank you, and please; and just because you said it, it was far from being settled in his heart. This, therefore, resulted in his journey being very, very difficult without the power of honor.

Consider the Contrast

Who was more beautiful than Mother Teresa? Her spiritual beauty shone through in such an amazing and wonderful way from the Christ like nature that the world saw in her as she demonstrated the power of honor.

Honor, therefore, is a decision which follows the laws of the Ten Commandments.

Commandments relating to honoring God (Exodus 20:3-8):

Thou shalt have no other gods before Me.

Thou shalt not make unto thee any graven image, or any likeness of anything that is in heaven above, or that is in the earth beneath, or that is in the water under the earth.

Thou shalt not bow down thyself to them, nor serve them: for I the LORD thy God am a jealous God, visiting the iniquity of the fathers upon the children unto the third and fourth generation of them that hate Me; and showing mercy unto thousands of them that love Me, and keep My commandments.

Thou shalt not take the name of the LORD thy God in vain; for the LORD will not hold him guiltless that taketh His name in vain.

Commandments relating to honoring people (Exodus 20:12-17):

Honor thy father and thy mother: that thy days may be long upon the land which the LORD thy God gives you.

Thou shalt not kill.

Thou shalt not commit adultery.

Thou shalt not steal.

Thou shalt not bear false witness against thy neighbor.

Thou shalt not covet thy neighbor's house; thou shalt not covet thy neighbor's wife, nor his manservant, nor his maidservant, nor his ox, nor his ass, nor any thing that is thy neighbor's.

There are, on the face of this earth, men and women who have come in contact with the reality of the transforming Word of God. These are those who have not chosen the path of dishonor, vain glory, an emphasis of self, extreme conceit, and exaggerated arrogance. Those of us who have chosen to receive Christ as our Savior and live the definition of honor. Our lives exemplify submission, service, virtue, and wisdom. Our reward is the impartation that stands us in the stead of Christ for the whole world to see. Our countenance, our conduct, our conversation, and our honor one to another become the very reflection of God's honor toward us, and in us.

God's Honor in Us

Hebrews 2:6-7, NKJV: *...But one in a certain place testified, saying, what is **man,** that thou art mindful of him? Or the son of man, that thou visit him? You made him a little lower than the angels; thou crowned him with **glory** and **honor,** and didst set him over the works of thy hands.*

We know clearly from Hebrews that God crowned us with glory and honor. We, then, have to make a decision to honor God, and honor people. We must also know and believe in the honor the Lord has imparted to us and **in** us. Honor is not vain glory. It is not an emphasis of self. In fact, extreme conceit is manifested by boasting, exaggerated arrogance, and name-dropping. All of this is better known as pride.

Pride usually happens directly before a person fails or falls. Many of our bitter trials, tests, and chastenings in life are because of the Holy Spirit's discipline against pride. The Lord and the Giver of Life has come to chasten us and bring us to a point in our lives where we are willing to do His will. So, do not waste your sorrow when you ask, "How long are these trials going to go on? Why am I not succeeding?" God's response would be, "When it doesn't bother you anymore, the victory is yours."

God's honor in our spirit is unconditional. The Bible teaches us that our spirit and the Spirit of God are one (Hebrews 2:11). While the Spirit of God in us is sinless, our intellect, reason, and emotion are not in agreement with God until our soul has been renewed through the washing of the Word of God. We press toward that goal that aligns all of us with all of Him.

The Concept of Seed

Biblically, Judah is referred to as praise (Genesis 29:35). The wonderful part about praising God is that spiritual praise plows the soil of our soul so deeply that our hearts are then open to receiving the engrafted Word of God. Yet, some still stand in self-righteousness. Rather than putting God's righteousness on and honoring God by speaking what He says about us, we choose to express our own traditional beliefs and actions which benefit no one and dishonor God. We must come to realize that only by taking off 'the old nature' and putting on 'the new nature' can we honor God (Colossians 3:9-10). Everything of eternal value you are ever going to get, you get by confessing the Word of God. Honoring God, honoring people, and accepting God's honor toward us is a decision that we make.

In order for us to perfect or bring things in our lives to maturity, we have to understand honor. The seed for success is honor. A seed must be planted and die before a harvest can be expected and soil is where all of this happens.

God's Adorning

There is no need to exaggerate God's righteousness by saying how good, great, and wonderful we are by trying to put on what I call "God facades" to make us acceptable. The Lord says; *Give your best to the Master.* He also says; *I can take the ugliness out of you.* This is divine adornment. If the wisdom of God is on you, your face has no choice but to shine. *Who is like a wise man? And who knows the interpretation of a thing? A man's wisdom makes his face shine, And the sternness of his face is changed.* (Ecclesiastes 8:1, NKJV).

Because the glow of God is on your face as the light of His wisdom adorns and honors you with His righteousness, you have no need to concern yourself with how pretty, ugly, or negative you may feel. If God says you are a head and not a tail, why do you call yourself defeated? If God says you are healed, delivered, and prosperous, why do you call yourself sick and down and out? What you plant, you will reap. **We are called to speak well of ourselves and honor God by agreeing with what He says about us. Life draws life.**

Honor Draws Honor

What you honor, you draw to yourself. For example, when we hear about the Ten Commandments and one of them says, *You shall honor the Lord thy God with all your heart,* your job is to be willing to believe His Word and say, "Lord, I honor you with all of my heart." You will quickly discover, then, that the Father will reciprocate.

I believe the root of all sin begins with dishonor and causes you to miss the mark.

One of the Ten Commandments also tells us to *"Honor your father and mother,"* which is the first commandment with promise: *"that it may be well with you and you may live long on the earth.* (Ephesians 6:2-3, NKJV).

Some may begin to ask, "What if my parents are not honorable?" Dishonorable parents have nothing to do with you giving them honor. Some may ask, "What if they have abandoned me? What if they were not good examples? What if this happened or that happened?" God decided where you would come from, and who you would come through, and He says; "Honor them." The difference between honor and obedience is discussed later in this book.

Honor is a Choice

We have to learn that honor is different from wisdom. Wisdom is the ability to use knowledge skillfully; to discern right from wrong. Wisdom shows us what is of God, and what is of the devil. The fear of God is the beginning of wisdom (Proverbs 9:10). Wisdom and honor, however, are two different things.

Honor is the willingness in your heart to reward another even though they are different.

Romans 12:10: *Be kindly affectionate one to another with brotherly love;* **in honor preferring one another.**

Nobody is "better than another," but we are "different than others." When honoring people, you honor their age, and their being. You condescend to men of lower estate without being condescending. **Honor is a choice that you have to make**. When we begin to see God's image in one another, the result is a preferring of others in amazing ways.

The law of honor is one of the most important laws on earth. Honor is not an anointing. It is a decision. Once you know you are the righteousness of God and that your life is hidden in Christ, you can afford to be magnanimous with anybody. You do not have to be threatened by what somebody has or does not have. Flaws are a part of human nature. There is not a family on the face of this earth that does not have dysfunctional qualities in it. We find dysfunctional qualities even in the lineage of Jesus as we examine His bloodline in the Book of Matthew.

Dysfunction Does Not Disqualify

Matthew 1:1-6: *The book of the generation of Jesus Christ, the son of David, the son of Abraham.* **Abraham** *begat Isaac; and Isaac begat Jacob …. And Solomon begat* **Boaz of Rahab;** *and Boaz begat Obed of* **Ruth;** *and Obed begat Jesse; And Jesse begat* **David** *the king; and David the king begat* **Solomon** *of her that had been the wife of Urias...*

Abraham had a heathen background and married his half-sister. Boaz's mother was the former harlot Rahab. Ruth's nation of origin was birthed from incest, and Solomon was the result of a woman whose husband David killed.

Now that was a unique group of people! From this historical example we can see that in our weakness, God's strength is made perfect.[1] *God has chosen the weak and the foolish to confound the wise and the mighty* (1 Corinthians 1:27).

---

[1] 2 Corinthians 12:9

Romans 7:19-25: *For the good that I would I do not: but the evil which I would not, that I do. Now if I do that I would not, it is no more I that do it, but sin that dwells in me. I find then a law, that, when I would do good, evil is present with me. For I delight in the law of God after the inward man: But I see another law in my members,* **warring against** *the law of my mind, and bringing me into captivity to the law of sin which is in my members. O wretched man that I am!* **who shall deliver me** *from the body of this death?* **I thank God through Jesus Christ our Lord.** *So then with the mind I myself serve the law of God; but with the flesh the law of sin.*

There is a war within our members. There are things that we do that we do not want to do, and there are things we do not want to do that we do. *O wretched man that I am, who shall set me free from the body*, that is, the bondage of this flesh? Read the answer in the next verse. *I thank God through Jesus Christ our Lord.* **Praise God who has made me free.** While we sometimes still feel the residue of the old nature, it has no power or authority as long as we choose to identify and honor the Word of God above what we feel and what we see.

It is written in 2 Corinthians 2:14, *Now* ***thanks be unto God,*** *which* ***always*** *causeth us to* ***triumph*** *in*

11

Christ.... Study, and choose to agree, with the Word of God.

Honor All

We often find ourselves surrounded by people that may not hold to the values we hold to as far as our faith is concerned. These people could be of great esteem; iconic people who have done marvelous feats as far as the world is concerned. It should not be a challenge to our faith to honor these individuals.

1 Peter 2:17: *Honor all men. Love the brotherhood. Fear God. Honor the king.*

We are here to love, encourage, exhort, and serve them. Yes, to serve them. There is nothing more detestable, frustrating, or limiting than arrogance. Never evaluate people by their experience or by their passion, but rather evaluate them by what and who they honor. Watch how people behave. Watch how people give honor to others. I decree that through the authority of the name of Jesus, we do have the power to honor all.

When honor begins its work in us, it elevates us, and surpasses every challenge.

Every time you begin to give honor, you will be elevated. Begin to say honorable things to yourself, and to the people in your life.

Keep Good Company

1 Corinthians 15:33 NKJV: *Do not be deceived: evil company corrupts good habits.*

A Prophetic Declaration

"He that walks with wise men shall be wise, but he who keeps a companion of fools shall be destroyed. Right now, in the authority of the name of Jesus, every fool in your life, the Lord extracts from you. You will not, you will not be ensnared by foolish people. You can be nice to everybody, but you should not be a companion to foolish people. Those who dishonor God are contagious. Every seed reproduces its own kind. Stay with wise people, those who fear the Lord. Those who fear the Lord, they shall rise up and their face will shine with the glory of God."

Make a choice to be with people who encourage and celebrate you, not just tolerate you. Separate yourself from those who are toxic, who abuse you, are fault-finders, who demoralize, belittle, and humiliate you. Choose not to keep company with people who incapacitate you by always having something negative to say about everything you do and every place you go, and whose ideas are always better than yours.

The Scripture says; *Without faith, it's impossible to please God.*

We are made in the image and likeness of God. The people that are going to edify you are people that have faith towards you and see your humanity, but are not moved by it. There is a godly correction that does not bring rejection. Correction is a good thing; corruption is not! Thank God who paid the price for all of our sins, and who has made us as righteous as Himself. What an incredible God we serve! We have to understand that there must be diligence in showing honor. We have to practice it.

"While I know myself as a creation of God, I am also obligated to realize and remember that everyone else and everything else are also God's creation." — **Maya Angelou**

Practice Honoring

1 Samuel 2:30: *… The LORD says … them that honor me I will honor, and they that despise me shall be lightly esteemed.*

When we come into God, we learn that dishonor is part of the old rebellious nature that refuses to listen to Him. When we refuse to listen to God through other people and we carry the attitude that asks the question, "Who died and made you king?" the outcome of your chosen path will result in a very, very difficult journey. As I related earlier, such was the case of the young boy I spoke about in my introduction. I am pleased to say that it is no longer that way, that he has come to have a very personal relationship with his Lord and Savior, and lives an honorable and godly life! The reality is that every person you see has a deposit of God in them.

Everybody is made in the similitude of God and the price for everybody's redemption has already been paid by Jesus, the Son of God. Has everybody activated that redemption? No. Judicially, it has been done. Experientially, it has not been activated by everyone through faith in Jesus Christ, the Son of the living God. However, when you and I are standing as ambassadors of Christ, our countenance, conduct, conversation, and the way we honor one another reflect that redemption in the face of all people.

Dr. Tandie Honors All

I have observed from traveling with Dr. Tandie, my Executive Assistant, that she does not make war with anybody but rather honors everyone regardless of their age or status. It is part of her human nature. She has been trained to honor. Honoring has become a part of her being. She ministers life wherever she goes simply by treating others with honor.

Children of Honor

While the first four Commandments center on honoring God, the fifth Commandment to honor our parents is basic to all other social relationships and foundational for a decent human society.

Children learning to honor is very important. When we honor our parents, we are honoring God. Our natural parents are a type of our Creator since they were God's agents in our creation. We should lovingly recognize that God chose our parents to become the natural cause of our life in this world. It is a righteous and proper principle to honor, love, and respect them. The Lord's intention is that the family would be a representation of His relationship with His redeemed. Genesis 1:27 teaches us that God created both male and female in His own image, so the pattern continues and children are to regard their parents as divinely ordained and truly significant.

The way your children respectfully treat you and others, and talk to you, relates to honor. Help them understand that honor not only causes them to be exalted, but extends to them the promise of long life.

Dishonor and disrespect are forms of unbelief that deny that others were created in the image of God. There are those who are ignorant of God's Word and His providential work in the creation of all things. Some rebellious people try to justify their wicked atrocities against their fellowman.

Devotion to one's parents is a sign of respect shown to one's culture and core values to ensure the perpetuation of both. Honoring your parents ensures that the future generations will know and accept the teaching of their elders. God has a perfect plan and purpose!

Reciprocity of Honoring

You will have a different relationship with those who honor you than those who dishonor you. Those who sow into your life with goodness should not be taken for granted. Those who do kind things for you and believe in you should expect reciprocity. It is much more than just a part of life. Someone honoring you is a gift from God. Wherever you find people who honor you, reciprocate with kindness. Learn to pay it forward.

We make a choice to believe good until it is proven not to be. Honorable people should be honored. The elderly should be honored. The simplicity of Scripture instructs us to stand when the elderly enters a room and, in that simple gesture, God is honored. Leviticus 19:32 NKJV, *You shall rise before the gray headed and honor the presence of an old man, and fear your God ....*

Misplaced Honor

If you have many children, you will love them all. God loves all of His children. Some of His children are more loveable than others! In the parable of the prodigal son, he says to his father, 'Because I was born in the family, I am entitled to certain things. Give me what I have not worked for and let me do whatever I want to do with your money and what you worked to get, because you owe it to me.' In today's culture, we see the spirit of entitlement running rampant.

This is the society we live in today and is what I call the "other side of the coin." We live in a time that glorifies evil and dishonors those whom God commands us to honor. Dishonor is everywhere. "Just give me what I want," they say. Disrespect

18

and mockery are a standard form of humor in our culture. Although Jesus experienced this reproach, His love overcame evil with good. He knew when to cleanse the temple and rebuke evil-doers. We are called to follow Christ, but there are many facets to His love.

We cannot assume a fatalistic resignation to the evil rule of the wicked; parents, employers, believers, leaders, civil servants, and anyone else that is dictatorial over mankind. It is not a Biblical imperative to honor or respect unscriptural violations of our mental, physical, and spiritual heritage. Sometimes, we are called to fight for our faith.

You are not to participate in anything that violates your conscience or that tolerates abuse. Honoring does not mean that you cannot confront or set boundaries on abusive and unscriptural behavior. God never rewards evil. We are not to honor evil teachers and preachers as evidenced by the inherent evil in Jim Jones and David Karesh. We are not to obey and submit to evil rulers and authorities, or abusive parents who are not deserving of honor.

The Bible is written to instruct godly people with godly principles. These principles cannot be applied to those who choose to be abusive, disobedient and rebellious. You should not treat a godly person the same way you would an evil abusive lawless person. We have become a society that tolerates almost anything. Scripturally, children are taught to obey, and adults are instructed to honor. A natural breach occurs, however, when evil attempts to cross the line of core values and conscience.

Honor Brings Favor

Honor is an amazing thing. It becomes like an airborne virus when you begin to activate it in your own life. You inhale and exhale the breath of God, and by modeling honor and respecting others with your countenance, conduct and conversation, people see how to treat others, and how to be treated. When you see a husband and wife talking to each other, there should be honor in their conversation. One should not tease, belittle, or uncover the other in any way. Ephesians 5:4, NKJV: *...neither filthiness, nor foolish talking, nor coarse jesting, which are not fitting, but rather giving of thanks.*

Because we are the bride of Christ, we should never say things that would dishonor the Lord. We should have no actions or activities that would dishonor our husband the Lord Jesus, our King and Savior.

As we honor the Lord and others, favor comes to us. We see that example in how some parents honor their children differently. The children who honor their parents are the ones the parents are more apt to encourage. They are all your children, and they are all loved. Yet, the ones who honor you are really the ones you are going to be quicker to encourage.

You must understand that favor is not necessarily fair according to human computations.

Money and Debt Free

I have these two little dogs named Money and Debt Free. Money is so polite and honoring. She is so humble and wants to be included but will never press. She just waits. If you put her up on the bed, she will run to the end of the bed and put her little head down. She is not going to press.

Then there is Debt Free. In the morning she runs in, jumps on the bed, gets on my chest, looks in my face, and wakes me with a lick on the nose. She is ready to play. She is jumping all over the place with the fullness of expression. She comes boldly into the presence of God (allegorically speaking)!

I love both of them very much, but it seems like Miss Debt Free is pretty cute and full of animated expression. I think about how God delights in us when we go public with our honoring and come boldly into His presence saying, "I love You. I love You. I love You. I love You." There is something about our jumping around before the Lord as we honor Him with our words and deeds that causes Him to reciprocate with rewards!

My husband will look at my little dogs. Money will come and sit at his feet and just look at him as if to say, "Could I please have a treat?" She will then stare him down. Miss Debt Free does a dance, spins around, rolls over on her belly, and will do whatever needs to be done to get his attention. She knows that somewhere in that bag there is a treat, and she knows that if she stays before him long enough, he will eventually weaken!

There are two incredible stories related by my friend Judy, both of which are wonderful expressions of the favor of God that accompanies one whose life exemplifies honor.

Judy's House Story

"A few years ago, I was building my own custom home and it came to the week prior to closing. It was on a Monday. I was notified by the mortgage company that told me all along through the building process that everything was great but, on the Monday morning before the loan was to close on Friday, they called me and told me what my payments were going to be. They also told me that my interest rate was going to be 11 ½%. I was anticipating 5 to 5 ½%. I could not afford to close the loan because my payments would have been

22

more than double. Immediately I went to prayer and I felt very strongly through counsel that I needed to have a second opinion on the mortgage loan. I sent the whole package to another mortgage company and asked them if they would just please look at my loan? I asked if they could do the loan at the 5% rate. The rates at that time were around 5 ½%. They said they would look at it. Later that day they called me and said, "Yes, we can close on Friday but you have two things on your credit report." No one had revealed to me before that there was anything on my credit report that would cause a problem.

They said, "If you will take care of that, we will be happy to close on Friday." I said, "Well, great! Just tell me what that is and I will take care of it." They said, "You owe $58,000.00 to the State of Arkansas in taxes." I almost had heart failure because, I thought, there is no way, $58,000.00? They continued with, "You also have a credit card that you owe $7,000.00 on. If you take care of both of those, we will close on Friday." That brought my total debt to $65,000.00. That night I prayed and asked God to grant me favor. The next morning I called the Tax Office of the State of Arkansas. The amazing thing was; I got through. Not only did I get through, I got through to the right person the first time. The lady I talked to pulled my file and said, "You have a business in the State of Arkansas that was never closed out." I knew I had gone through the proper procedure to close it out. The lady went back through the file and said, "Well, wait a minute. I see where you did close it out and it was never documented." She said, "You know what? I'm just going to take your file before the Judge and ask him to just stamp your file cancelled, paid in full." I asked her, "How long will it take you to do that?" She replied, "Maybe 30 minutes." I asked her if she would please fax me a copy of it that showed the Judge having signed off confirming that the debt had been cancelled and was paid in full. Within 30 minutes I had a fax from the Tax Office of the State of Arkansas confirming that $58,000.00 of back taxes had been cancelled and was paid in full.

Then I got on the phone to the credit card company. Someone had taken out a credit card in my name and charged $7,000.00. I never even knew that I owed this. The bill was four years old. I talked to the representative at the credit card company who said, "Yes, ma'am, you do owe this." When I explained to her that I did not even know about it, she said, "Well, you know what? Because it has been so long, I am going to stamp this debt cancelled, paid in full." Within 24 hours, all of the debt was cancelled. I was able to close on Friday. When I went to the mortgage company with all of the documentation showing that $65,000.00 in debt was cancelled and paid in full, they were overwhelmed and asked me how I got all this cancelled. They said, "First of all, how did you even get through to the right person at the State Office? When you call those people, it takes sometimes weeks to get something like that handled. How did you do this?" I looked at them and said, "It is called the favor of God." They said, "No, really, really, how did you do this?" I said, "Seriously, it is the favor of God." I was able to close my home loan as scheduled on Friday because of the favor of God."

Judy's Airport Story

"I arrived at the airport that I was scheduled to fly out of. When I got there, I found out that my luggage was 10 pounds overweight. I looked at the gentleman checking me in at curbside and said, "Sir, I am asking you for favor." He said, "It's going to cost you $100.00 to get this luggage on the flight." I said for the second time, "Sir, you have the ability to grant me favor." He just shook his head and left. When he came back he said, "You need to go inside with me, but when we get in there, keep your mouth shut, because I've got this."

We got to the counter and the agent told me, "We can't check your baggage in because you're at the wrong airport." I was just startled by that and said, "Ma'am, surely you can get me on a flight from Houston to Dallas sometime this afternoon." She said, "Well, that's going to cost you $200.00." I replied, "Ma'am, all I'm asking you for is favor." The curbside attendant was standing behind her and said to me, "Don't say another word." I did exactly as he said!

She started looking for another flight for me and said, "I don't know what just happened but, are you willing to pay $10.00 to change your flight?" "YES!" The curbside agent put the tags on my luggage, and just looked at me. It cost me $10.00 to change my flight, instead of $200.00. He looked at me as he was putting my tags on and said, "It's called favor." I said, "And we both know favor isn't fair." He responded, "Absolutely." I said, "Sir, you have been so kind to me today because what should have cost me $300.00 cost me $10.00. May I pray for you and your family?" He agreed, "Absolutely." So right there where you check in, I stopped and prayed for the gentleman. I moved along only to get to the gate and find out that there were about six other people who all ended up in the same situation I was in; at the wrong airport. Once again, I found myself ministering to all the distraught people that were waiting at the gate.

When I got home, I discovered that something had happened to my computer. At the instruction of technical support, I took my computer back to the store for repair. The lady at the repair desk told me, "It will cost you $500.00." I had not even had it a year yet. I looked at her and said, "Ma'am, all I am asking you for is favor. I need favor." She left the room, went back to talk to the manager, and was gone for a very long period of time. When she came back she said, "I don't even know how this happened but the manager approved a replacement at no cost to you." So, within 24 hours, what should have cost me $800.00, cost me $10.00 because of the favor of God. You have not because you ask not. I had asked for favor, and I continue to do that, and could tell you story after story after story. Favor, favor, favor."

Lucifer,[2] a son of Honor

One of the interpretations of Lucifer's name means the son of honor. His job description was to gather all the honor from the angelic hosts and pour it before God. When he saw God receiving all the honor and all the glory, he said, 'I will ascend to be as the most high God.'

Isaiah 14:12-14: *How art thou fallen from heaven, O **Lucifer**, son of the morning! how art thou cut down to the ground, which didst weaken the nations! For thou hast said in your heart, **I will** ascend into heaven, **I will** exalt my throne above the stars of God: **I will** sit also upon the mount of*

---

[2] A name used by Jerome to define the word Heylel (morning star) in Isaiah 14:12 and other places in both the Old Testament and the New Testament.

the congregation, in the sides of the north: *I will ascend above the heights of the clouds; I will be like the most High.*

He became conceited with pride. How did the iniquity of dishonor enter in? Ezekiel alluded to Lucifer's dishonor of God by referring to it as the multitude of his iniquities and the iniquity of his traffic.

Ezekiel 28:17-18: *Your heart was lifted up because of your beauty; you hast corrupted thy wisdom by reason of your brightness: **I will cast you to the ground,** I will lay you before kings, that they may behold you. You have defiled thy sanctuaries by the **multitude of your iniquities,** by the **iniquity of thy traffic...***

God responded to Lucifer's dishonor by advising him that he would not ascend. *"You shall be brought down to hell, to the sides of the pit* (Isaiah 14:15). There comes a time when you must separate from those you have given a place to in your life who dishonor you. As the lightning flashed in the sky, God said, 'I thrust him out with all of his friends.'

Luke 10:18: *And he said unto them, I beheld Satan as **lightning** fall from heaven.*

Revelation 12:9: *And the great dragon was cast out, that old serpent, called the Devil, and Satan,* *which deceives the whole world: he was **cast out into the earth,** and his angels were cast out with him.*

Do not allow people to dishonor, abuse, and misuse you. You are royalty. You must understand that meek is not weak; it is strength under control because you are the righteousness of God. There were three distinct angels that had divine authority and territorial power. They were leaders. When leadership is given to anyone, honor must be released in the midst of the job description.

Michael, Gabriel, and Satan each had a different purpose that they were to perform in order to bring honor to God. However, Satan forfeited his honor and was cast out. There is something in all of us that is competitive in nature. Even Paul tells us to run to win, not run to run. Our competition, however, is not against others, it is against our self. Herein lies our need to accurately identify our enemy. Scripture tells us we will know them by their fruit. Honor those things that are honorable by examining their proven fruit.

Understand that delegated authority is supposed to produce honor to God. You have been delegated to be saviors and bring glory and honor to God. Be like Michael and Gabriel by honoring the Lord in fulfilling your purpose in Him.

Saviors

You have been anointed and appointed to stand in the stead of Jesus, the Son of the Living God. You have been created to be **saviors** in this world; to heal the sick, cleanse the lepers, raise the dead, and cast out devils.

Matthew 10:8: *Heal the sick, cleanse the lepers, raise the dead, cast out devils: freely ye have received, freely give.*

Obadiah 1:21: *And* **saviors** *shall come up on mount Zion to judge the mount of Esau; and the kingdom shall be the LORD'S.*

Nehemiah 9:27 NKJV: *Therefore you delivered them into the hand of their enemies, who vexed them: and in the time of their trouble, when they cried unto you, you heard them from heaven; and according to thy manifold mercies you gave them* **saviors,** *who saved them out of the hand of their enemies.*

You do not get a chance to have a bad day. Every day with God is honorable; all the promises of God are yes and amen. Honor is a decision. You cannot inquire of the flesh because the flesh will say, "I am hurt, wounded, getting old, and am down and out." On the contrary, strengthen yourself with the joy of the Lord. Do not reach for the phone, reach for the throne. Begin to open your mouth, chew on the Word, and believe.

$\mathcal{Y}$ou have been
delegated to be saviors
and bring glory and honor
to God.

The Sound of Honor

Romans 10:17-18, NKJV: *So then faith comes by hearing, and hearing by the word of God. But I say, have they not heard? Yes indeed, their **sound** went to all the earth, and their words to the ends of the world.*

Honor carries within it a certain sound, a resonance and a vibration, a frequency of like things that begin to speak to each other. There are people who hear, really **hear**, my voice when I say something profound like, "Hello." There is the sound of honor that comes from us as we speak kind words to others. Those good things God has stacked up in us will suddenly go down inside of others as we speak to them in honor. They will hear and say, just like the woman at the well, 'I met a man that told me everything I ever did.'

We know He did not tell her everything she ever did. He said, 'Woman, the man you are with now is not your own.' Husband number seven, Jesus, the Perfect Man, was standing before her. He had not told her everything she ever did. He said only one thing but, from her perspective, He had told her everything. This is the domino effect. The sound of honor that came from Jesus resonated in her. Therefore, she wanted to honor Jesus. As a result of the sound of honor she heard in Him, she evangelized her entire city!

There are those that have the ability to hear, fear, and honor the Word of God; take it, and run with it. Some people have to hear it repeatedly before they do anything. Others hear it one time and they are off and running. There is a sound; a sound of honor. Honor can be taught. It is not an anointing. It is not a gift. It is a decision. You decide what you will honor. Remember, what you honor, will come back to you.

The Angels Hear

Ecclesiastes 5:6: *Suffer not your **mouth** to cause thy flesh to sin; neither say thou before **the angel,** that it was an error: wherefore should God be angry at your voice, and destroy the work of your hands?*

Dishonor is not only contagious, but disqualifies you for reward. The Scriptures are clear that ministering spirits sent forth from God to help us who are the heirs of salvation heard that conversation! God's response to that is, 'How dare you touch My servants!' Learning how to order our conversation to be righteous should be among our top priorities in life. *"Unto him that orders his conversation righteously will I show the salvation of God"* (see Psalm 50:23).

Honoring Leaders

Honor is the seed for access into any environment, in any season.

Acts 23:5 *You shall <u>not</u> speak evil of the ruler of thy people.*

Honor those who are in authority; child to parent, student to teacher, employee to employer, citizen to political position. It does not matter that you do not fully understand them. They are different from you specific to their position of authority. You do not have to agree, but you do have to honor. What and who you honor will come back to you.

In every situation we must honor. 'He's not this, and she's not that.' God is the just judge. He knows exactly who is where and sometimes places people in our lives just to see how we will respond in the season of frustration and antagonism. Will you stand fast and make the declaration of the Lord, or murmur and complain because you do not understand what is going on and why it is the way it is?

It is here that I must make a disclaimer that is significant enough to be repeated in subsequent pages of this book with regard to honoring those in authority. There is a significant difference between honoring and obeying. The Scripture says that the honoring of those in leadership and authority will result in things going well with us. A leader who is ungodly is not worthy of obedience. Daniel comes under the auspices of, and serves with incredible honor, four heathen kings. The Bible says Daniel honored their office "forever." Whether he was in their presence, or in another location, he could be trusted to carry the honor of their office wherever he went and with whomever he was with.

Joseph waited in prison for the Lord to elevate him. When the king sent for him, the Bible says he shaved his beard and shaved his head. By taking on the look of Egypt, Joseph honored the one who was in authority.

Scripture clearly commands us to "first" pray for all those in positions of leadership and authority and speak well of them. Your disagreement with a leader or one in authority does not prevent you from honoring the position. If one in authority is morally inept and doing things that violate your conscious, your body, or your moral convictions, there is no obligation on your part to be in their company or submit to their leadership.

Honor transcends culture and condition.

You Speak Right Things

Ephesians 4:23-24: *... And be renewed in the spirit of your mind; and that **you** put on **the new***

man, which after God is created in true righteousness and holiness.

Remember, everything you are ever going to get from God, you will get with your mouth by confessing and agreeing with the Word of God.

Proverbs 18:20-21: *A man's belly shall be satisfied with the **fruit of his mouth;** and with the **increase of his lips** shall he be filled. Death and life are in the **power of the tongue:** and they that love it shall eat the fruit thereof.*

Our new nature is righteous and speaks righteousness and life. It is holy and speaks right[3] things because God created us in true holiness. Therefore, we honor God by saying what He has said about us. God spoke everything into existence. He did not blink it. He did not think it. He spoke it!

Genesis 1:3; 6-7: *And God **said,** Let there be light: and **there was light**... And God **said,** Let there be a firmament in the midst of the waters, and let it divide the waters from the waters.... and **it was so.***

---

[3] Note: The word used for holiness in Ephesians 4:24 is a Greek word that literally means "intrinsically right;" hence, "holiness."

Release the Word of God to Eliminate Condemnation

Ephesians 6:14 says it this way so beautifully, *Stand, having girded your waist with truth, you must put on the breastplate of righteousness.*

The only way you are going to guard your heart is by sounding the truth of God's Word. With your mouth, you put on the breastplate of righteousness. Though your heart may condemn you, God is greater than your heart and He instructs you to put on the breastplate with your words. It is not a chest plate. The breastplate is where love and faith nurture and must be based in His righteousness, rather than your self-righteousness. When God looks at us, He filters us through the blood of the Lamb of God that takes away the sins of the world.

The Lamb's Blood Speaks

John 1:29: *The next day John sees Jesus coming unto him, and says, Behold the Lamb of God, which takes away the sin of the world.*

Hebrews 12:24: *And to Jesus the mediator of the new covenant, and to the blood of sprinkling, that **speaks better things** than that of Abel.*

The Lamb of God taking away our sin is enough, in and of itself, to warrant honor. The blood of Jesus not only speaks to us, but over us. We honor God by saying the same things He says, 'What you honor, you draw to yourself.' By honoring God, you are drawing God to yourself. If you honor the Holy Spirit, you are drawing the Holy Spirit to yourself. It is so important to understand this principle. Because God is inside of you, He does not find fault with you.

Ephesians 1:4: *According as he hath chosen us in him before the foundation of the world, that we should be holy and **without blame** before him in love....*

The only way to protect your heart is to guard it from condemnation. There are a lot of voices out there telling you that 'you are never going to make it, there is something wrong with you, you did not do this right, or you did not do that at all. Why aren't you someplace else at this time in your life? Why haven't you accomplished this? Why haven't you done that?' Have you heard voices like that before? Feel free, through the weapons of God, to cast down those imaginations and say to those voices, "Devil, why don't you just shut up? I am not going to allow condemnation to come into my mind!"

2 Corinthians 10:4-6: *(For the weapons of our warfare are not carnal, but mighty through God to the pulling down of strong holds) Casting down **imaginations,** and every **high thing** that exalts itself against the knowledge of God, and bringing*

39

into captivity every thought to the obedience of Christ; and having in a readiness to revenge all disobedience, when your obedience is fulfilled.

Fruits of Righteousness

Philippians 1:11 says that we are *being filled with the **fruits** of righteousness.* Not fruit; fruits; *the fruits of righteousness, which are by Jesus Christ to the glory and the praise of God.* We are exhorted to think on whatsoever is lovely, whatsoever is true, whatsoever is virtuous, whatsoever is praised, and so on (see Philippians 4:8). You can break it all down to this. **It is the kindness of God that causes people to come to know Jesus** (see Romans 2:4). It is not how smart you are or how talented you are; it is how much love is in you to honor others. You must release that love of God.

You are filled with honor wherever you go. The love of God is shed abroad in your heart because what you honor you are drawing to yourself. God becomes your healer as you refuse to be ensnared in any attempt to try to heal the old nature. You cannot do it alone. It is a study in futility. You simply have to "be" who God says you already are.

How many of us have ever said, **"I am not going to eat that piece of pie?"** After everybody has gone to bed, you find yourself being drawn to it and, after having eaten it, you hear a condemning voice in your mind saying, "Well, if you had any willpower, if you had character, if you had integrity, you would just be able to say no." Once we confess our sin to Him and repent, we find that God looks at us and filters us through the blood of the Lamb of God and the Spirit of God who is in us. God gives us strength to resist temptation if we honor Him by yielding to Him.

We are trying so hard to do well instead of be good. We do have to learn the discipline of self-control. God says we are filled with the fruits of righteousness. If, in this flesh, there are things that I do and say that are not consistent with the Word of God, I must then choose, by faith, to honor God's Word and thank Him for the discipline He is working in my life.

Hungry for His Life

Have any of us ever earned anything in God? Everything any of us have that relates to God's life has been a gift. It is often when we are at the worst in our actions that God does the greatest things in our lives. When we eat from the Tree of Life, we are strengthening the new life God has given to us. This occurs when we are truly hungry for Jesus. There are times we find ourselves looking in the refrigerator, or looking in the closet; looking for something without knowing what.

The truth is we are really hungry for something from God that has not yet touched our souls. There is something inside that is driving us to be filled with His life. We have read all the books and sung all the songs, looked at this, and looked at that, yet, there is something telling us there is another dimension and that we were created for something bigger and better than this. We know there is a place in God beyond where we currently are.

With God all things are possible (Mark 10:27b). Once we come to believe that we are as righteous as God, and that nothing has been laid to our account except righteousness, holiness, and deliverance, we can come to expect to win every battle and find that place in God beyond our present circumstances.

Righteousness by Faith

My true righteousness is the righteousness which is from God by faith. This good news is almost too good! Philippians 3:9 says, *And that we be found in him,* (a wonderful preposition) *not having my own righteousness* because our own righteousness is from the law. Our righteousness is through faith in Jesus Christ. We almost invariably want to do something to earn His righteousness. You have heard people say, "He learned all the steps, but could not do the dance." There are people I know that do everything right but never learn the dance of life and have no idea what honor is all about. They never learn about loving, forgiving, or passion. They do not understand that humans do and say things that are inconsistent with the nature of God so God says to them, 'Because you could not do it, I did it for you.'

God's Strength

Having a clear understanding that God does things for you has to make you happy! Movies are filled with characters that have incredible willpower. In some movies, the characters are being dunked in water, or sawed apart in an attempt to extract information from them. In the midst of that hardship, they hold on.

In the natural, whether fact or fable, few of us would be so determined! Yet, through God who strengthens us, we are able to do things that are beyond our strength. Anything and everything that is good and strong in us is all of God. Be encouraged today, as you finish reading this book that, as you continue to be 'found in Him,' impossibilities do not exist!

Honor begins with you; the honor you have for yourself. You see, until you can love and honor yourself, you really cannot love or honor anybody else.

Loving Yourself

Galatians 5:14: *For all the law is fulfilled in one word, even in this; you shall love thy neighbor **as** yourself.*

You love and honor yourself by choosing to forgive yourself. In this life, you are going to have trials and tests, but temptation is not sin. Sin is the result of having yielded to the temptation.

Talking about forgiving yourself, this reminds me of my wonderful friend and the legendary, Dr. Iverna Tompkins. She is an inspiration with limitless information that brings transformation to the lost and humiliation to the rebellious. Her Biblical accuracy, laser wit, and prophetic insight is a triple braided cord that lassoes wild horses, brands the Lord's herd, and scares off all predators. She continues to set the bar with her queenly appearance when she enters the room!

Dr. Tompkins puts it this way, "When the day comes in our lives and we feel that all have forsaken, or worse, that we have turned on ourselves because no one can hate you as fervently as you. No one can hold a grudge against you quite as well as you can against yourself. Something that the Holy Spirit does is take the reality of it and bring it down to your desolate heart and say, "You must forgive yourself." His love for you would compel you to forgive yourself. God is looking for men and women who are without rancor not only about others, but about themselves. His fervent love and expression begins with deliverance. Psalm 71:2-4 says, *Deliver me in Your righteousness, and cause me to escape; Incline Your ear to me, and save me. Be my strong refuge, To which I may resort continually; You have given the commandment to save me, For You are my rock and my fortress. Deliver me, O my God, out of the hand of the wicked, Out of the hand of the unrighteous and cruel man.*

A 'flash from the flesh,' a thought that is akin to road rage, appears out of nowhere! Recognize it as temptation, discern its origin, and counter-attack with the Word of God. Let Philippians 4:8 which says that 'whatsoever things are lovely and pure and true,' *if there be virtue, and if there be any praise,* these are thoughts that are of God, be your battle cry!

Prophetic Exhortations

"Transformation! You have seen the bitter, but you shall soon know the sweet. You know the fragmented, but now you shall soon know the complete. There is a raging champion inside of you that is crying to be released. You have fought with the shield of faith. You have fought with the shield of faith. This day, says God, "I take the shield and say hold it. Hold it."

The day has come that now out of your mouth shall come the double-edged sword of God and you will say, "It is written. It is written." It is written and I shall lift you up out of this miry clay. I put a crown upon thy head and a scepter in thy hand.

Come out. Come out. I take the grave clothes off of you. "You are created for signs and wonders. You are created for magnificent things," says God. "You shall no longer be held in deception of the old nature, but I call you holy. I call you forgiven. I call you blessed and empowered."

You have keys, and destiny is in your life. You will not be concerned with what other people say; other people's opinions and thoughts and ideas. You are not a man pleaser. You cannot be a man pleaser. You will not try to please man from this day forward." The Lord says, "Free, free, free, every area of opinions of others that have dishonored you, I move them," says God.

The voice of God will be heard in you. The voice of God, the Lord says, "It is not you that chose Me, but I, the Lord God, have chosen you. I have destiny upon you and you shall be a defender. You shall be a defender and it will not be with your fists. It will be with your mouth," says God. "Where there are bullies, I am going to give you the antidote to bullies," says God, "and you will stand." And when you see people that are not being treated right, I shall rise up like a giant inside of you and you will look to this person and say, "Don't do that." And there will be consequence in your mouth,"" says God. "There will be consequences with your words."

"Why does it have to be so hard? I have seasoned you in the fires of affliction, in the crucible of the opinions of others. Two steps forward, ten steps back. Two steps forward, ten steps back."

God is marking you for honor. May the supernatural unction of God that is in your life be released to a new power!

Who will agree with God? Who says I am holy? Who says I am righteous? Who says I am healed? Who says I am delivered? Who says I am wealthy? Who says I am righteous? I am filled with honor. I choose to honor those who are different from me in color, in condition, and in culture. I choose to be a life-giving spirit. I am through with being threatened or intimidated by what I have or have not manifested. I am redeemed. I am a child of God. There is more to me than what you see. I am totally equipped to do exploits for the glorious King and His glorious kingdom.

Prophetic Poetry

"Listen, listen, listen, listen, listen and hear
Listen to Me say that I'm who you'll fear
You will open up your mouth and you'll prophesy
And where it's been thirsty and the people have been dry
You will release such a flood
Listen to the Word of God, plead the blood,
Release the Word, the power and the truth
Open up your mouth
And turn God loose in your secret place
In your secret place
Mercy and grace
Must be released
Because you are a king and a priest
In your closet you are going to prophesy
You are going to activate and ratify
Clap your hands and dance all around
Open up your mouth and give Me a shout
You've got to shout with clout
You've got to shout with clout.

Come up here and see what I see
Come up here and create with Me
From My vantage point arise
I'm not God just up in the skies
But I'm living in the midst of your very breath
This is the season you are going to enter in
God's rest, God's rest," says the Lord.

Declaration:

I decree that there is a redeemed remnant that has activated and embraced the revelation of the new creation reality. With the words of their mouths, they have "put on" Jesus, the transforming Word of God, and they have "put off" the memory of the old nature. These are those who are spiritual and not religious, and by faith they have chosen to agree with God!

I hear an army of anointed words cleansing the earth. They are the voices of many waters; the many-membered body of Christ releasing the voice of God that freely flows from the bellies and out of the mouths of the overcomers. I proclaim the Kingdom of God is a kingdom of words; Holy words, powerful words, healing words, restoring words, all rushing out of the voice activated people of God to renew the earth. Can you hear the inaudible, see the unseen, smell the unscented, taste the tasteless, and touch the untouchable? You are a candidate to opening wide your everlasting gates that must release the glory of God.

I declare that a divine intervention of God's glory has begun. I hear a new vibration. It is a certain sound that imparts a supernatural witness. It is an ancient, timeless sound to stir an eternal knowing within the "heavenly species." This sound causes the overcomer to experience a metamorphosis and creates an atmosphere of glory and honor in and out of this earthly realm.

There is an awakening to the overcomer's destiny to administrate the estate of God and comprehend the power of the Law of Honor!

Spontaneous Prophetic Song by Dr. Clarice Fluitt

How will you know?
How will you know a wise man's in your midst?
His face will shine with glory divine.
How will you know, how will you know?
Crowned with glory and wealth
Crowned with glory and wealth
Wise men in this house
You've got a miracle in your mouth
Activate the Word of the Lord
Move by faith in one accord.
Don't look back to yesterday.
Hear the voice of the great Yahweh.
Listen to the Word and now is the time.

You're not carnal, you're awesome and divine.
Nothing's going to get any better for you
Until you believe that you really are new
Who would agree with God?
Who would agree with God?
Now is the season as never before
Listen to the Word of God, He'll tell you what's in store.

About Dr. Clarice Fluitt

Dr. Clarice Fluitt is an internationally recognized Christian leader, accomplished businesswoman and entrepreneur with a history in real estate development. She is also a much sought-after Motivational Speaker, Personal Advisor, and Certified Transformational Life and Leadership Master Coach.

Her high impact speaking engagements at Lead and Succeed Business Seminars have joined forces with other speakers that include Suze Orman, Bill Cosby, Larry King, Les Brown, Michael J. Fox, Steve Forbes, Rick Belluzzo, Daymond John, Shaquille O'Neal, and other legendary speakers. These innovative and supercharged events provide individuals with proven methods, formulas, strategies and keys that skyrocket individuals to higher levels of success.

She is a time proven prophetess with laser like accuracy. Reports of amazing miracles and healings with positive life changing evidence continually follow Dr. Fluitt's ministry. Dr. Clarice's life is a remarkable chronicle of hilarious real-life stories, tragic trials, tests, and moving visitations of the Lord. Unpretentious and friendly, she is a highly esteemed minister and conference speaker.

Other CD sets we recommend:

- Seeing the Invisible Clearly
- Secrets of My Prayer Life
- Invading the Marketplace
- Don't Give Up Your Dominion
- Healing Everywhere
- Moving On
- They Didn't Meet on Facebook
- The Sovereignty of God
- The Believers Job Description
- The Mentality of an Overcomer
- Awaken to God's Love
- Setting Clear Boundaries and Keeping Them

Ministry Contact Information:

Clarice Fluitt Ministries
P O Box 7888
Monroe, LA 71211
Phone: 318.410.9788
E-mail: claricefluitt@claricefluitt.com

Websites:

www.claricefluitt.org
www.claricefluitt.com

31627307R00040

Made in the USA
San Bernardino, CA
15 March 2016